TRAPPED IN THE PAST NO MORE

Trapped In The Past No More

Escape from a place laden with negativity and hurt into a space of peace and freedom

Erick Matthews

Copyright © 2020 Erick Matthews

Cover design by Jarrod Walker

All rights reserved. This material is protected by the copyright laws of the United States of America. This material may not be copied or reprinted for commercial gain or profit. No part of this publication may be reproduced or transmitted in any form or by any means, electronic or mechanical, including photocopying, recording, or placing on the Internet, without written permission from the author.

If you would like permission to use material form the book (other than for review purposes), please contact gumbomediaproductions@gmail.com. Thank you for your support of the author's rights.

Scripture quotations are taken from the King James Version Bible © 1979, 1980, 1982 by Thomas Nelson, Inc. Publishers. All rights reserved.

First Edition: August 2020

ISBN: 978-1-7353994-0-9 *(Paperback)*
ISBN: 978-1-7353994-1-6 *(Digital)*

Printed in the United States of America

DEDICATION

I would like to dedicate this book to my grandmother, Geraldine Givan of Birmingham Alabama. She's gone on to be with the Lord but has left behind a legacy of many people who have been impacted by her life. She has literally shaped my thinking and prepared me to process the experiences that would eventually lead me to write the book. There were so many times you crossed my mind while writing this book. As I recall all the wisdom you have given me during the time you were here, I'm more than confident that people will be impacted by this book like your life impacted me.

This book is also dedicated to my older sister Deshawn Givan. I'm sure that you and granny are having a wonderful time in heaven. I love you both forever.

Table of Contents

INTRODUCTION	1
Chapter 1	*3*
Learned Behavior	3
Chapter 2	*9*
Perception	9
Chapter 3	*14*
Value and Truth	14
Chapter 4	*20*
Healing Change and Time	20
Chapter 5	*25*
Operating in The Now	25
Chapter 6	*29*
On Your Mark, Get Set, Go	29
Chapter 7	*35*
The Break Out	35
ACKNOWLEDGEMENTS	39

INTRODUCTION

I would like to talk to you about being trapped in your past. This is a problem that most of us can identify in the lives of others but more than often it goes undetected in our own life. Past relationships, past experiences, and past decisions all play a major part in how we act, what we do, and what we believe. Could it be that how you react to problems that occur in your life create a certain way of thinking? Well, it is what you think and how you respond to life that can and will create a reality that you can't escape from unless you begin to respond and think differently about life. This reality can be a negative world, where most of your life you experience problems, disappointments, hurt's and pain. It can be a world where almost every person that you connect with brings about a negative impact in your life. Although positive things can and will happen what you believe if negative creates that reality.

On the other hand, if your thought process is a positive one, I believe that your reality will be positive. Negative things can and will happen in life but your positive thinking and response to life will create a positive reality for you. I believe that the reason for this is that the way you respond and think acts as a magnet drawing, attracting, and making negative or positive deposits into your life. The Bible says in Proverbs 23:7 **"so a man thinks in his heart so is he"**. Another version says, "**so he becomes**". That's right, the power of your thoughts pulls experiences into this realm.

So, as you read this book beware of the fact that you are responsible for your thoughts and actions. Understand that your past can only live in the present if you speak about, think about, or meditate on it. For example, thinking about past pain will bring the pain of the past into the present. In fact, most people are living in a time warp. They constantly allow what has happened in their past affect their present and shape their future. They leave one relationship only to meet the same person with a different face. Others block themselves from progress because of distrust, bitterness, or hatred. Many are still stuck in a moment where they have experienced pain or disappointment and are somehow unable to get over the trauma of that moment although it happened many years ago.

This book is going to show you how to escape a life rattled with negative events that like a sitcom rerun plays on the screen of your mind repeatedly. It's going to teach you how to control your thoughts, which will help you control what you say. In addition, it will help you to control your actions and change your habits. Finally, it will help you to identify your purpose and chart out your journey to reach your destiny. It will also help you position yourself to live a life free of moments and events in time that can hold your peace and happiness hostage and prohibit you from living a life of serenity. Later, in this book I will share with you some powerful examples of these truths. But first let's talk about the root of the problem *"Learned Behavior"*.

Chapter 1

Learned Behavior

For most of us our problem can be traced back to the things that we encountered as a child up until now. It is called learned behavior. Learned behavior is developed through the observation of statements and actions in your life and in the lives of others. A wise man once said if you want different results you can't continue doing the same things. Often, we use old solutions for new problems and try to fix spiritual problems with natural solutions. We come up empty handed, frustrated and ultimately hopeless thus causing us to settle into an *"it will never change mindset"*. This paradigm eventually causes one to develop a habit of trying to live under conditions that he or she doesn't have to live under.

Unfortunately, we as humans sometimes go a whole lifetime adjusting to life instead of making life adjust to us. How you think will shape your whole life. *In fact, the condition that your life is in now is a result of a collection of words, spoken by your mouth, thoughts that came from your mind and actions performed by your body.*

Children are exposed to this behavior at an early age and develop the same response, inherit the same mental mind set thus shaping their lives to a certain reality. Finally, after years of learned behavior convinced that there is no way out one begins to kick into what is known as survival mode.

When we grow older and take on the responsibility of caring for ourselves just like a computer accessing a file saved on it's hard-drive our mind recalls the same decision and response of generations past as a possible solution and the saga continues. The same decision and response introduced to our parents by their parents is chosen and becomes a perpetuation of experiences that are synonymous with the past. It infiltrates the present, and echoes in the future causing a chain reaction that locks our bloodline into a vicious never-ending cycle of misinformed decisions and obscure perspectives. Survival mode causes you to give up on any hopes of ever living stress free in that area. You just simply learn to live with the pain never having a break but eventually settling into a dull, consistent agony that you become immune to after a while. You offer no resistance because at some point it becomes natural to live under those conditions.

Survival mode dictates to you how you should respond to problems that occur in life. It teaches you how to accept the conditions of life when God created you to change the conditions of your life, and not submit to whatever life throws your way. **Life will not change as a favor to you. You must change your life as a favor to it.** That is to say that there are people in life that need to see you change your life so that they can change their life. Listen my friend, God wants us to live a life free from the bondage of depression, sadness, disappointments, etc. He desires for us to break out of the past and change the direction of our lives to reflect the true intention of why he created us in the first place *"**Dominion**"*.

God created us to rule over problems in our lives and not have problems rule over us. We were all created by God and given the ability to create a reality full of good things from health to wealth. Regardless of what we are exposed to as children there is a certain mindset that acts as our enemy or our foe. Thus, ultimately, we can't blame anyone for our quality of life. If we are going to blame someone, then we must blame ourselves. You can't help what has happened to you as a child. However, you can help how you move forward with your life as an adult. We must obtain knowledge that frees us from the past to create a wholesome now. Negative learned behavior and the lack of knowledge serve as a veil that blinds us from the true perspective of life. They couple themselves together as parents to foster a child, called *"mentality"*. Mentality develops and grows into something that can help or hinder you during life. It does not matter what your mentality is, when it fully matures it will produce after its own kind be it good or bad.

Expose yourself to knowledge and wisdom. Because the only way to do better, is to know better. Many of our mistakes came because of us being misinformed. We knew what was right but didn't make the right choices, or we just didn't know at all. However, we can choose to learn from the behavior of past mistakes, or we can learn from obtaining knowledge that will cause us to avoid some of the pitfalls of life. Mentality comes from wisdom, knowledge, and experience.

We must take the knowledge that we have gained from our experience and the experience of others to escape having to grapple with the same cycles throughout our lives. As long as our mentalities remain the same, our quality of life will remain the same. But, as soon as your mentality changes, by default things around you will begin to change. This is the mystery of life. You can live a life free from the fear of going through the same thing your parent's and loved ones went through because of bad decisions. Getting to where you want to be starts with a choice, then a commitment. There is a difference between making a choice and committing to the choice you made no matter what.

Making a choice requires committing to see change. But you must embrace change. Change can sometimes be extremely uncomfortable. However, if you can push through being uncomfortable it can yield some awesome benefits. Always remember that growth and maturity require change. There's no way you can get around it. When you grasp that things can change and you can change them, your mentality has begun its journey of maturity. Wisdom is the application of knowledge and will help to mature your mentality. ***After fully maturing, mentality gives birth to perception.*** And perception is needed to apply wisdom accurately. You've heard it at one time or another. What you see is what you get!

Notes

_____
_____
_____
_____
_____
_____
_____
_____
_____

Questions

What are some negative learned behaviors you to need to change?

_____
_____
_____
_____

What survival techniques do you use?

_____
_____
_____

What knowledge and wisdom are you exposing yourself to?

_____
_____
_____
_____

Thoughts about this quote: *In fact, the condition that your life is in now is a result of a collection of words, spoken by your mouth, thoughts that came from your mind and actions performed by your body…*

_____
_____
_____
_____

Chapter 2

Perception

Perception is the way we view life. It is a known fact that you can't go no farther than what you can see or believe, from a physical or spiritual perspective. Understand this statement because there is certainly more than one way to look at life. You can look at life through the lenses of the natural realm which projects a very dull and unclear reality, or you can choose to look through the lenses of faith in the spiritual realm that gives you the ability to see things that others may not be able to see.

To be limited means the point, edge, or line beyond which something cannot or may not proceed. It also means a confining or restricting object, agent, or influence. To put it in plain terms our interactions with objects, agents, and influences should not confine or restrict us from learning how to take control of our lives. Looking through the lenses of faith frees you from the limitations of the natural realm. It causes your way to be made clear. It is through the imagination and the confession of your mouth mixed with work that will produce the reality that you desire according to the will of God. In that context seeing is believing. It has been proven that what we see is easier to believe than what you can't see. Often, we as humans are not able to get past a problem because that's what we look at and focus on. What we should be looking at and focusing on is what God said about us and our situation. To believe means to accept as true and real.

Whatever you except as true and real governs your life. Because we believe in the law of gravity, there are certain things we won't do. Because that law governs our life, we won't jump out of a plane without a parachute or step off a ten-story building and expect to live. What I'm trying to say is that you should see yourself free from the cares of this life and confess with your mouth that you're free. Let that reality govern your life. The bible says, "Faith cometh by hearing and hearing by the word of God'. Find out what the Word of God says about your quality of life and begin to see and confess that word over your life. Every time you think about it, begin to confess and I assure you that things will change for the better because that will become your mentality. After it matures fully it will give birth to your reality through your perception. There are major and minor lessons that can be learned in life. One of the keys is to major in minor lessons.

The way to major in a minor lesson is to pay close attention and give detail to every lesson. Learn everything you can from the situation, and you could avoid a major mistake in the future because you learned a minor lesson. It is those lessons that change your perception in life so that you see clearly what needs to be done to bring you to the place of your desire. If you are going to look back in the past it should only be to remind you of the value in those lessons that came from what you encountered in the past. It should be those lessons that become your personal mentor when making decisions for the future. Experience is a powerful teacher.

The more that you focus on the pain that your mistakes caused the more you will feel the guilt and disappointment of your past in the now. This causes one to become trapped. What are you becoming because of your thoughts, actions, and habits? Is that what God intends for your life? When you value and focus on the lessons you learned in life it causes you to avoid lots of potential mistakes in the future. You should not lean to your own understanding but in all your ways acknowledge God and He will direct your path. The value in knowing your worth is priceless. Knowing your value helps you to look at life through a different pair of lenses. It also helps others to see your true value. Take some time and get to know yourself beyond what people feel or think about you. Get to know what you like and dislike, what makes you happy or sad, things you love to do etc.

Getting to know you is important and vital not only to relationships with others, but a wholesome relationship with yourself. If you don't know yourself, you put your love at risk of being trampled over. No one will know your true value until you know who you are. How you treat yourself is how others will treat you. Always remember, people treat you how they see you. Therefore, it is extremely important for you to understand the truth about your value. And you will never discover your value with the wrong perception.

Notes

_____
_____
_____
_____
_____
_____
_____
_____
_____

Questions

What confessions do you speak over your life?

_____
_____
_____
_____

What areas do you need to change your focus in?

_____
_____
_____
_____

What makes you valuable?

_____
_____
_____
_____

Thoughts about this quote: *Whatever you except as true and real governs your life...*

_____
_____
_____
_____

Chapter 3
Value and Truth

Every chapter in this book is important but this one is vital to your success in life, relationships and anything you may face. Sometimes we as humans allow problems to decrease our value. We cheapen the value of who we are by how we respond to life, choices we make, and the mental state that we allow ourselves to dwell in. Thus, it gives us a distorted picture of who we are. Gather yourself for this next statement because this may catch you off guard. God wants to introduce Himself to you through you. He wants you to become exposed to the truth about who you really are.

The word value means of great importance, having admirable or esteemed qualities or characteristics. You are a part of Him, and He is a part of you. That makes you of great importance and value. The Creator is the most important thing in this world. But what happens when the most important thing is put in a place? That place becomes the most important place. Can you phantom this?

The place that The Creator has chosen to reside is in you, which makes you the most important place. It is in this place that God desires to introduce himself to you and to others. Acts 17 and 28 teaches us that it is in him that we live, move and have our being. However, 1 Corinthians 6: 19-20 reveals that we are the dwelling place of God. So, we live in him, but he also lives in us. What a wonderful thing to know that the most powerful presence that has ever existed chooses to exist in us while allowing us to exist in him. The awesomeness of this reality should overwhelm you. That divinity would share the same space with the mortal, that Infinity would spend time with the finite, that the unsearchable would allow the simple to find him.

It is a disservice to ourselves and to the whole human race that we would live our whole lives never discovering these truths. Yet, The Most High impressed upon my heart to reveal this to you. There is no where you can go that God is not. In-fact God is never on his way anywhere because He fills all space. This means he is everywhere at the same time. Focusing on his presence consistently, reveals who we are. The longer you focus on God the more you begin to reflect who He is, thus discovering who He has created you to be.

Knowing who you are gives you an opportunity to have a wholesome relationship with yourself. It teaches you how to break out of the vicious cycle of dysfunction and treat yourself with respect and dignity. This is especially important because people usually treat you how they see you. If you do not see yourself as valuable and important how can someone else see you as such.

The truth of the matter is when you seek to understand your identity from the Creator, He will reveal to you who He is first. You will then begin to see yourself in him. It is at this point that you must be courageous enough to respond. Respond with your soul. Your soul is your mind which consists of your thoughts, your emotions which is how you feel, and your will which is your ability to express how you feel. This will completely alter your personality. Your personality is just a combination of your thoughts, what you feel about them and what you express as a result. Understanding who you are will cause you to think different thoughts, feel different emotions, and expressed differently then you have in past times, liberating and freeing you from the person you were before this truth was revealed to you. This will introduce a kind of care and self-love that will be delightful too experience to say the least.

God is love and when you mirror that people are drawn to you. God even draws us through his love and kindness. It is only when you know the truth about yourself that you will be able to identify truth in others. The truth in you will call out to the truth in someone else. The truth is the light and when you see the light you should walk in the light. That light is revelation. Have you ever heard someone say, "I see what you are saying in a whole different light"?

Revelation is like a type of ex-ray vision that gives you the ability to see past the false and identify the truth. Sometimes we as humans are not able to handle the truth because the truth can be something, we are not ready to accept. However, the truth is necessary for without it we cannot see things in true light or revelation. Learn to accept the truth whether it is in your favor or not and it will cause you to experience freedom like you've never known. It is especially important that once you find the truth that you accept what is and embrace what isn't. Sometimes the truth is hard to swallow but it is necessary. In addition, there is something else that is required.

You must let go of your false beliefs, mentality and perceptions of the past. Whenever the truth is revealed, if accepted then and only then can your healing begin. If there is a misconception it is usually found in the soul which is the mind, emotions, and the will. But your spirit is open to truth. It is forever ready for you to assume your rightful place. The Word of God is a sword that cuts and divides the truth from a lie so that you can clearly tell the difference between the two. It is important to consider that healing will never take place in an individual's life if one does not embrace value and truth. Because it takes an understanding of value and truth for healing to take place and for one to be freed from the past.

Notes

Questions

When you think about your identity what comes to mind?

How do you see God?

What do you do to practice self-love?

_____
_____
_____
_____

Thoughts about this quote: *The longer you focus on God the more you begin to reflect who He is, thus discovering who He has created you to be…*

_____
_____
_____
_____

Chapter 4
Healing Change and Time

There is a period that you will enter after you have become aware of your learned behavior, obtained the right mentality and perception, understood your value, and have become exposed to the truth. Healing must take place. Because before you can break free of your past you must heal. Healing changes your reality with time. The pain does not end until you heal completely, so you need time to heal. When you are truly healed, the past is forgotten until needed. This is a wonderful stage to enter. At first it can and will be extremely hard to make the adjustment but as time passes it will get easier. Healing is a stage where the disappointment, pain and hurts begin to fade and the excitement about life is restored.

In this period, you can look back at your negative past to pull out the positive lessons learned at that time to ensure that you will not make the same mistakes. It is the freedom from the past that brings healing into play and allows you to enjoy this present time without being trapped in the pain of your past. There are several ways to discover that you are healed. Some include but are not limited to being able to talk about whatever it is and not feel the pain it caused. Being able to meet the person, or be in the place, and not feel uncomfortable just to name a few.

That painful time in your life will not have a negative effect on you when you refuse to keep it alive in your memory any longer. When you are completely healed you will only reflect on the past to glean from negative experiences that yielded positive lessons. There is a certain way a person carries themselves when they are healed. These people are sure of themselves, cautious but not suspicious. If they have gone through a complete process of healing, they will respond differently than they have in the past to problems that life may present. In the process of healing something wonderful begins to happen. A transformation begins to take place. There will be a noticeable change in that person who has gone through the healing process. I believe that change is the ultimate test in life. It can be extremely hard to change things after doing them one way for so long. But there will come a time in everyone's lives where things will change. People, places, and things will change as well as yourself. There is a time for all things. There's time to laugh and a time to cry. There's a time for happiness and a time for sadness.

There is a time to live and a time to die. Without change there is no growth. Without growth there is no maturity. Without maturity there is no clarity. When there is no clarity it can become incredibly stressful. Thus, time becomes the real test. Most of us would be fine if we were dealing with a problem in our life and when things would be fixed or get better. But often time becomes the issue rather than the test or trial that we are facing. I know that I'm going to make it out of this! But how long will I have to wait, when is my change coming, when will the hurting and pain stop are the questions that come to mind.

Someone said that time heals all wounds. I don't know if that statement is completely true. Healing doesn't take place until you forgive and move away from the past. You must stop investing mental energy and what happened and what devastated you in the past. Until then you are only hurting yourself and apprehending your ability to live a life of freedom from past behaviors, decisions and emotions. You must concentrate on the now! Ask yourself what is right now? What is okay now? Become extremely grateful for the answers that are revealed because of those questions, because they will serve as key's that will unlock your emotional prison and introduce you to a life of intentional living.

To want means to feel that one needs. But it is the power of gratitude that brings to you what you've become grateful for. Often it is what we want that causes us to be limited. What we want is most of the time different from what God knows we need. What you need is what you should be focused on. A need is necessary and mandatory for your life. So, focus on what you need because when you get what you need you can always get what you want. We need a word from God. We need His direction. When we get direction for our lives then we can navigate through life seamlessly.

Notes

_____
_____
_____
_____
_____
_____
_____
_____

Questions

What areas of your life need to be healed?

_____
_____
_____
_____

What lessons have you learned from your pain?

_____
_____
_____
_____

What is your plan to get free and stay free from the bondages of your past?

_____
_____
_____
_____

Thoughts about this quote: *When you are completely healed you will only reflect on the past to glean from negative experiences that yielded positive lessons...*

_____
_____
_____
_____

Chapter 5

Operating in The Now

Your past present and future should not be equally important. If everything is important then nothing is important. I am not saying that your past, present, or future should not be important, but I am saying that they should be on different levels of importance. You distinguish the importance of multiple things by prioritizing. What gets the priority over something else determines the level of importance it has? Your past cannot be changed or altered. It is a record of human existence that is based on decisions that you made at that time. Whatever those decisions produced by way of consequence are hard facts. The good news is that a wholesome now can be created and intentionally experienced using the data collected by observing the dynamic of decisions made in the past. Analyzing that information to craft new decisions that will produce positive results will afford you the opportunity and God-given privilege to create your own life experience. You can't experience healing in the now if you are shackled by the heart shattering memories of the past. Because your past becomes your present when you insist on mentally hanging out there. Rather take advantage of precious moments that are happening as you experience life.

By far now should be more important than the past or the future. The past and the future borrows from the now. Neither can be spoken of unless it's spoken of now. You have the wonderful option of choosing to live in the now as opposed to being tortured by the pain of the past or pimped by the future. The Illusion of the future is that things will eventually get better, but the power of the present is that things are already better, you just must realize it. Acknowledging and embracing this truth allows you to fully operate and experience the power of the present.

It's like an eyeball focusing on an object. The more that the eye focuses on the object, the pupil begins to dilate taking in more of what it is viewing. As it continues to focus and refocus, it loses its peripheral abilities to see anything other than what it is focused on. When we set our attention on the now with such intensity, we will ultimately lose focus of the past and future and just enjoy the now. The more the focus, the more the intensity, until a glimpse of happiness turns into a world of happiness.

Notes

_____

Questions

What are you focusing on right now?

_____

What are some plans you have for your future?

_____

What are some obstacles you have overcome in your past?

___

Thoughts about this quote: *The Illusion of the future is that things will eventually get better, but the power of the present is that things are already better, you just must realize it. Acknowledging and embracing this truth allows you to fully operate and experience the power of the present…*

___

Chapter 6
On Your Mark, Get Set, Go

There is a mark in life that we must find. Our goal should be that God helps us find that mark. The mark is a place that God has designed especially for you. It is not intended to be your last stop. It is in fact your starting point. Your mark is a place that God has designed for you to start doing what he wants you to do. Finding this place gives you the advantage you need to start in the place that God has for you. It is your launching pad so to speak. Remember it is always a struggle for you to get on your mark. This is the place that will catapult you into your destiny. Paul says in Philippians 3:14 I press toward the mark of a prize of the high calling which is in Christ Jesus.

Remember the mark is not the finish line it is the place where you start. There will be a press or resistance trying to get to the mark because the mark places you on the path for the prize. It is the prize you want but first you must get to the mark. Many of us press for the prize but not from the mark or place that God wants us to start from. When you start from any other place than the mark your press is always harder than it would be from the mark because on the mark there is grace for you to press. There is no grace to press for the prize if you are not on the mark. Even when you get on your mark there is yet another step that you must take before you can move forward. You must get set. To get set means to prepare. You must get in a position to take off.

There will be no time to prepare when it's time to go. What I am saying is that you must get on your mark and get set to go before you go. Preparation is especially important know matter what stage in your life you are in. The reason why is that if you're not prepared to go to the next level, chances are you will be stuck in your past. Sometimes God allows things to come into our life to prepare us for the next level. If there is poor preparation, there will be poor application. If there is poor application there will be poor manifestation and if there is poor manifestation, there will be poor appreciation. One must learn to appreciate where he or she is before they can move on to another level. Let's not forget that there are valuable lessons that can be extracted from our present situations that will literally be the catalyst for our next levels. How many times has God given us things that we did not appreciate therefore the lack of appreciation kept us stuck in the past? The past should not have precedence over now because it now represents new opportunity.

Sometimes the things that we take for granted must be taken away from us to appreciate what God has done. If there wasn't sadness, we would not appreciate happiness. We as humans don't appreciate things until they are threatened or taken away. After you have prepared yourself there will come a time where you will be released to begin the race. You must remember that when you begin the race there will be all kinds of things coming against you to stop you from finishing. One of the first things that will come is discouragement. This attack often comes through relatives, close friends, or just people in general. Most of the time they are not even running in the race. They are on the sideline trying to discourage you from running the race.

Essentially, they become distractions that can slow you down making your journey longer or cause you to stop all together. The goal of the enemy is to get you to waste as much time as possible. There are windows of opportunity that we must take advantage of in a certain amount of time or that opportunity will pass. Chance and opportunity come to every man, but it is always moving, and we must get on our mark to take hold of it. If we can stay focused and not listen to people on the sideline there will be other things that will try to stop us. There will be hurdles in our way that we will have to jump over or go around to finish the race. When I began to think about this, I asked myself the question "What is the purpose for the race"? Then finally the answer came to me. The purpose for the race is so that you can change, thus making your problem or situation change. Notice that the starting point and the finishing line on a racing track are the same thing. When you start running the race you take off at the starting point. After running the race for a while, the sign changes to the finishing line. You are just running in a big circle, so the track does not change.

The track and the race are designed to change you so that when you come full circle you have a different outlook on the track and the race/life. Notice how the person that runs the race after finishing is happy and excited about making it back to the point from where they started. Life is a race that we all must run. When Adam and Eve fell from grace, they caused us to have to run a race that would eventually bring us back to the starting point. The purpose for the race is to change our perception and mentality about life so that it is the right one. There will be tests and trials in this life that will try to stop us from getting to the finish line, but Jesus came and ran the race because before he came no one who ran could finish it well. But because of what he has done it has afforded every human on planet Earth an opportunity to run this race well, starting with breaking out of our past.

Notes

_____
_____
_____
_____
_____
_____
_____
_____
_____

Questions

What have you been procrastinating in?

_____
_____
_____
_____

How do you need to prepare for what's next?

_____
_____
_____
_____

How do you handle resistance?

___

Thoughts about this quote: *If there is poor preparation, there will be poor application…*

___

Chapter 7

The Break Out

This final chapter is my gift to you in the form of an acronym. It is literally the key to being released from your past. The first letter in this acronym stands for "Begin". Before we can see results in any area of our lives, we must begin. Things don't end wrong, they start wrong. The first step you must take is to start over. You may think this is impossible because of the current consequences of past mistakes. Just forgive yourself and wipe the slate clean and start over in your mine.

You may have to deal with the consequences of past mistakes in a very real way, but you absolutely have a choice to live in the past or live in the now. So, choose to live in the now at this very moment but begin in a very intentional way. Start with the end in mine and know what you want your outcome to be. The next letter stands for the word rest.

Rest is essential to both the body and the mine therefore there must be an intentional schedule of sleep and rest, to refresh your body and you're mine. You must rest from physical activity as well as mental activity and allow your mind and body to reset. Your body and mine will both perform at optimum levels when given the tools to do so. The next letter in the acronym stands for elevate.

You must elevate your thinking by turning your life experiences into life lessons. These experiences must become lessons that will teach you what is necessary to thrive in life. The next letter in the acronym stands for always. Always be conscious of the thoughts that you are thinking and the conversations that are going on in your head. What you think about the most will keep you in the present or trap you in the past. The next letter in the acronym stands for knit. You must learn how to knit your conversations mentally, and physically together with what you believe.

This will produce corresponding behavior and deliver to you your desired results. The next letter in the acronym stands for occupy. You must learn how to allow positive thoughts to occupy the spaces in your mine that once incubated negative thoughts. The next letter in the acronym stands for utilize. Utilize these techniques on a consistent basis and form them into habits that cannot be broken. This will cause the technique to become failure proof.

The last and final letter stands for trust. You must trust what you're doing long enough to realize undeniable results that will come into fruition because of your relentless repetition. As I end this final chapter, I would like to thank you for taking time to read this book and offer you even more support by walking with you step-by-step through my mentorship and coaching program called B.R.E.A.K.O.U.T. This program will go into deeper depth and intense detail using 10 video presentations as well as a workbook helping you to break out of your past. These techniques have been tried and proven and are solely responsible for me breaking out of my past.

Notes

_____
_____
_____
_____
_____
_____
_____
_____
_____

Questions

What have you not begun that you need to?

_____
_____
_____

Is there something you need to start over?

_____
_____
_____

What tools do you need to be a success?

_____
_____
_____
_____

Thoughts about this quote: *You must elevate your thinking by turning your life experiences into life lessons....*

_____
_____
_____
_____

ACKNOWLEDGEMENTS

To my mother Helen Marie Harding who bares the grace that her mother and my grandmother Geraldine embodied, and continues to shape my thinking as it relates to family and ministry, I love you. To my wife, friend and business partner. Nothing is more comforting to know than you have my front, side, and back. I love you dearly

To Dr. Chiffon Foster, I am grateful for all the hard work you put into editing this book for me. I look forward to working with you on many more projects. Last but certainly not least I would like to thank Jarrod Walker. I want to thank you for your hard work and dedication on this project. Excellent job on graphics and I appreciate what you do that make things happen behind-the-scenes. I look forward to working with many more projects with you.